THE ONLY WAY OUT IS THROUGH

A Journey of Facing and Healing from the Hidden Truths Discovered

Angeline, Thank you for all of your support & always having my back. I love you. Love yourself first!!

By: Cindy Kaywin

Cindy Kaywin

Copyright © 2022 by Cindy Kaywin
Published through Rising Above Publishing Services

www.risingabovepublishing.com

All Rights Reserved.

This book is a memoir. It reflects the author's present recollections of experiences over time. The information shared in this book represents experiences lived through by the author. Some names and characteristics have been changed, but no events or characters have been fabricated. The advice and strategies discussed may not be suitable for every situation. This book is intended to be informational only and is not intended to replace legal advice.

Paperback ISBN: 9798448102509

Dedication

I dedicate this book to my children, Samantha and Jarrod. You have always been my light, my love, my heart, and I can't thank you both enough for being there when I needed you the most. I thank God that he allowed me to be your mother. If I taught you anything, I hope that you know that it's OK to love yourself first above all else, before anyone. I love you both with every ounce of my being!

I also dedicate this book to my mother. She was my hero; I couldn't thank her enough for loving me the way she did. Rest easy mom. Till we meet again. I love you!

INTRODUCTION

"

It will only break you if you let it.

Author Unknown

"

Was it me? Could I possibly be the one with the problem? Maybe I've lost my mind and I don't even know it. My thoughts were racing trying to piece together the craziness that had become my life, trying somehow, to still make sense of it all, as I sat in my car that winter day about to give up. Yes, I was ready to kill myself. As hard as it is for me to admit, it's the truth. I've always been the strong one; the woman who has taken letdown and betrayals time and time again and have not only moved on each time but have always come out on top; the woman who took care of everyone else, but this time was different. This time I had hit my limit.

My car was running in my closed garage, and all I could do was try to take deep breaths in between my sobs. "It'll all be over soon. It'll all be over soon", I whispered to myself with each breath. At that very moment, that's what I needed; I needed my reality to be over. I couldn't take one more minute, one more second of this pain. The overwhelming shame, humiliation, anger, and hurt from his betrayal was all that I could feel combined with the guilt for sitting in my car, not just contemplating suicide, but actually trying to, even though I knew I'd be leaving behind my children and mother.

Death seemed to be the only way out of this. I couldn't think of any other way to escape what I was experiencing every day, and I had gotten to the point of total mental exhaustion. I couldn't stop the events replaying in my mind, feeding my fear that he's going to do it again, and on top of it, I was made out to be crazy by him because I can't "let it go and forgive him" because he said he's sorry. "Is that what happens? Is that how this whole marriage thing works." I thought to myself.

His manipulation tactics even had me start second guessing myself and I kept thinking that perhaps something was really wrong with me because I couldn't let this go and forget about it. After all, forgiveness is what it takes to make a marriage work, right? All my life I've given great advice to my children, my friends, everyone else, and I've thrown the word forgiveness around like it's so easy. But there I was, completely incapable of forgiving my own husband?

What he did was too atrocious. Sleeping with other men this entire time we were together, sneaking around for all these years with random men he barely met online, even being paid to service them and more often, being serviced by younger men or "twinkies" as he referred to them as. The emails I had discovered months ago revealed a completely different man to me than the man I married. Yet, when confronted there was no remorse. Not even when I agreed to try to fix things by us going to individual therapy- still, no remorse. When I cringed and backed away from him touching me, he'd behave as if something was wrong with me. He acted as if he couldn't understand why I didn't want him to touch me or why he couldn't live with me. I was told that I'm acting crazy and need to get over it already.

I had become completely obsessed with stopping my husband from betraying me and even went as far as downloading an app that allowed me to see everything he was doing on his phone. I would sit in my office at work staring at my phone, watching his every move. I justified putting myself through this because I understood why he did the things he did- he had a serious problem. In therapy, it had been revealed that he had unhealed childhood trauma, but I didn't know if that was even real or not or if it was another lie that he dished out to me. All the things I've had to understand over the course of my life and marriages and, somehow, I've always been the one left feeling misunderstood, even in the midst of experiencing extreme betrayal.

I clinched the steering wheel as if it would pull me out of the depths of hell, I felt myself sinking to. I laid my head in between my arms on the wheel crying out loud to God for a sign, to be saved, for something to make sense. During my surrender, I could slowly feel myself coming back to me. "What am I doing? Why am I doing this?" I whispered to myself in between my cries. I lifted my head and caught a glimpse of myself in my mirror, and I didn't recognize this woman staring back at me. I didn't recognize her at all. She wasn't me, that's one thing I knew. "How did I end up here?" I thought to myself. I quickly turned the car off, my hands were shaking, and looked at myself one last time in my rearview mirror and told myself out loud, "He's not going to win. This is not going to beat you." That was the day all gloves were off. That was the day I decided to take my life by the reins and start healing from this toxic bullshit that continued to play out in different ways in the different men I married. That was the day I took my power back. This is my story of redemption that all started by discovering the truth.

CHAPTER 1

THE DEVIL IN DISGUISE

> When God shows you it's time to let someone go, and you refuse to accept it, God will allow that person to hurt you to the point where you have no choice but to let them go.
>
> **Unknown Author**

There's a proverbial suggestion that the third time is always the charm, while, ironically, the number three has also been associated with the devil. They say when the devil presents himself to you, he's disguised as everything that you've ever wanted. Coincidentally, or maybe not so much of a coincidence, on January 3rd, 2015, I met the devil himself- my third husband. If there was a picture under charming in the dictionary his picture would be right there. In a state of complete vulnerability, I was ideal prey for what I now can only see as a narcissist on a hunt. I was beyond tired, beat down by life, hungry for real, and in desperate need of love, not knowing it was really self-love my soul craved for.

Understanding my worth and seeing my value has really been an uphill journey in my life. It's required me to slowly lift the blindfold to salvage pieces of myself from each marriage, every betrayal, so that I can see who I really am in order to rebuild myself time and time again. I've been forced to learn hard lessons that pushed me to stand on my own two feet and keep going. I think a lot of us women somehow lose ourselves along the way, spending our energy trying to save broken men, trying to prove our worth to people that are not even worthy of us to begin with. I've learned that this is codependency at its finest, but before gaining this new self-awareness, I naively kept it moving, like I always do, never giving myself a break, and trudging my way with few boundaries and one big heart on my sleeve.

In 2015, I was three months officially out of my second marriage, a marriage I had emotionally and mentally checked out of six years prior. Yes, for six long years I had been strategically plotting my exit from that marriage in order to secure my financial stability. Because of my careful planning and patience, I was able to keep my properties and money when I did leave. I felt like I was finally free and ready to start living my life.

I had financial independence, which was something I definitely did not have after my first marriage, but I hadn't scratched the surface of the trauma that led me up to that point. I hadn't dealt with all the insecurities and issues that come from being married to someone that constantly belittles and verbally abuses you. But you don't know what you don't know, even though, so often we think we do. I know I thought I did, even when my children told me about their concerns of moving onto another relationship so fast. I found myself justifying my decision, over and over, desperately wanting to convince my friends and family that this time was different. I suppose all along I was really trying to convince myself. What I really needed was time for the dust to settle inside of me, to heal, so that I could clearly see what I wanted; for my life and from the people I allowed in it.

I hadn't felt free in years and mistaken it with me being ready to put myself back out there again and date. I purchased a membership on a dating website that screened their members and started talking on the phone for a few weeks with a guy that fit all the categories of being a decent human being. Our face-to-face meetup kept getting postponed due to different issues going on in both of our lives. Eventually we arranged our first casual date at a local bar. As soon as I walked in, he stood up from the bar that he was waiting for me at, and he wasn't what I was expecting. He was so big, a muscular man that towered over me at 6'5, with blue eyes and blonde wavy hair. His arms were covered in tattoos, and he rode a motorcycle. It felt like a breath of fresh air to feel safe with a man that exuded masculinity. And not just physically safe, but emotionally. Despite the "bad boy" appearance, he was so thoughtful and gentle to me in the beginning. When we were together, it was as if I was the only woman in the room. All his focus was on me. I was not used to that. I was not used to feeling seen or heard. That feeling outweighed any red flags that started appearing, and they started appearing fast.

I found it strange that on our first date, he took me to meet up with another couple who he was friends with, instead of us being alone to acquaint ourselves more. I found it strange that he didn't step in and say something to his friend who had made provocative remarks during a heated disagreement he initiated with me. I found it strange that he took me to Florida just two months after our first date to meet his parents. Red flag after red flag kept showing themselves to me, but I continued to only see what I wanted

I got along well with his parents, especially his beautiful mother. Everything seemed to be going so smoothly for all of us, it was like we just fit. That is, until after day drinking by the pool a few days into our trip, there was no denying the big red flag being waved right in my face that day.

His mother loved jellybeans and had a bowl of them on the outside table. We were tipsy from drinking in the sun that afternoon, but all our conversations were in good spirit and fun. We were having a light-hearted debate about what were the worst and best flavored jellybeans, and I proceeded to tell him that I can't stand the black ones.

"Have you ever had a black jellybean?" He quickly shot back.

"Yes, of course I have. That's how I know I don't like them." I said, still laughing.

"Are you sure you don't like the black ones?!"

"Yes, James! I don't like them!" I repeated, but as I said it, I could see a grave look come over his face and knew we weren't talking about jellybeans anymore. It upset and irritated me because I've never been one to play these games especially ones with racist undertones.

"You're sure you don't like the black ones?" He asked me again but a bit slower as if I didn't somehow understand what he was asking before.

"Actually, I have had black ones and they're pretty amazing." I said with a smile.

He gave me a look of pure disgust and quickly stood up and walked away while mumbling something under his breath to me. Right then and there I knew this was wrong. My plan was to leave first thing in the morning, but, of course, with the morning came sober James, and he said all the right things and had reverted to being the attentive man that I had quickly fallen in love with. He moved our relationship so fast. The only way I can describe what was happening is that I was being love bombed by what I can only now describe as a narcissist. I allowed it because I had never felt like I mattered up until this point; I wasn't healed. I allowed myself to be trapped in believing the prince charming on a white horse lie. It all seemed too good to be true, but I convinced myself that was the broken part of me that didn't believe I was worthy of real love. The inner conflict distracted me from seeing and accepting what was being shown to me.

When whiskey shots were involved, the jealousy and anger came out full throttle. What was supposed to be a romantic weekend getaway quickly turned to be a date from hell. We went to a nearby bar by our hotel, and while he was throwing back whiskey shots, I was making casual conversation about my job and what the day's events were with my coworkers who happened to be mostly men. Out of nowhere, he raised his voice loud enough for everyone to hear, "Guaranteed, they want to sleep with you! Have you slept with them?!"

Shocked and humiliated I whispered, "James, they are only friends. I've known them for the past eighteen years or so. They're like brothers."

As he was screaming out crazy accusations I walked out and headed back to the hotel to grab my things and requested my car to be pulled around. I was ready to leave him downtown, but he jumped into the car with me, and we went back to my house instead of the hotel. I made him sleep his drunken stupor off, and the next morning demanded that he leave. I wasn't about to let myself get caught up in another abusive relationship. I didn't talk to him for a couple of days and when I did finally answer his call, he blamed it all on the whiskey and, once again, promised up and down with tears streaming down his cheeks that he would never touch whiskey ever again.

He kept that promise, until we were married, that is. He proposed on May 30, 2015, and almost three months later on August 21st we got married. His behavior slowly started to change after we said our vows; after he knew that he had me. What I didn't realize was that the purpose of having me around was a cover up for something bigger than I could have ever imagined.

There was this side of him that was so attentive, so thoughtful, and caring, and it gave me a false sense of security while completely blinding me. It was the small things that spoke so loudly to me. When I would get a migraine, he'd call into work sick just so he could stay home and take care of me. Making sure I didn't slip and fall in the snow by putting one arm around my waist and holding my hand with the other. His hand was so big, it would engulf my small hand when holding it, and there was something about it that made me feel so safe. When he took care of me after my neck surgery that I had to have, he helped me with the normal daily activities and never left my side. Those little things slowly stopped, and I found myself yearning for the man that made me feel like I mattered.

It started off with just one whiskey shot, then "what's the big deal with a few". The next thing I knew he was bringing a bottle to a friend's house, and it was out of control from there. His behavior started becoming more erratic as time progressed and so did his drinking. I knew something was off and asked him several times to just tell me what was going on. So many scenarios were running through my mind. I knew he used to snort cocaine in his younger years, he used to tell me he partied like a rock star, so I thought was he doing drugs again on top of the alcohol? I never saw drugs or traces of drugs anywhere we went or in our house. Whatever it was, I knew there was something. No matter how hard I pleaded to him for answers, I'd always get the same response "It's nothing. I'm just stressed out from work." It never added up though, because I'd wonder what kind of stress could someone possibly have that works on the assembly line at a factory?

As if that wasn't enough, I soon realized that he was a chronic spender. Amazon must've been at our door every other day with something that he purchased, and never out of his personal account but always out of our joint account that was for our bills. When confronted, it was always an argument, he'd wiggle out of the real issue and yell at me that I made more money than him, and that he didn't have much spending money like I did. I never could get a straight answer to his spending habits, and not even Jesus himself would be able to make sense of it.

Then in April 2017 he had a heart attack, and it brought me to my knees. I had conversations with God like no other time in my life, praying not to take him from me. I stayed in the room with him the entire time, never leaving his side during his recovery. Every doctor visit, every doctor phone call, I was right there. I thought that this would help put him on the road to a healthier lifestyle. I hoped that he'd stop drinking and take better care of himself, but as soon as he was able to, he didn't miss a beat and got right back to it.

Like everything else, I let it slide. I've learned it's those gut feelings that we dismiss that we always end up regretting. I thought one day I'll learn my husband's secret, whatever inner turmoil was going on, and then we'll have to work through his addiction of alcohol. Never once did I think or could have possibly imagined what that secret was. My mind couldn't fathom such a thing, but I'd soon find out four years after being together, the lie that I had been living in.

CHAPTER 2

THE DISCOVERY

> *There are no secrets that time does not reveal.*
>
> — **Jean Racine**

Certain things thicken our skin to prepare us for our journey ahead. You get to a point where heart break doesn't feel like it'll ruin your entire life anymore, where the acceptance of loss has become easier, where saying goodbye still hurts but you've learned how to still go on. Yet, nothing in my life prepared me for Wednesday, August 28th of 2019.

My mom was terminally ill with cancer, and my siblings and I rotated shifts caring for her. For most of my adult life I've battled with anxiety, so even on my days off caring for her, I was unable to sleep and spent my night trying to shift my focus from the anxious thoughts and fears that always started bombarding my mind during late hours. Since my mom was sick, the anxiety had gotten worse, and consequently I was riddled with exhaustion.

My anxiety has always been something that no one in my life has ever completely understood. It's created this barrier if you will from anyone fully connecting with me. James was different though, at least in the beginning. He acted like he understood and showed patience with me and with how I had to do things in order to cope with my anxiety. Sometimes the order of which I get things done doesn't make sense to others, the extra steps or time in which it takes me to accomplish something takes longer than most people.

When I'm having an anxiety attack the most support I've been used to getting is being told to calm down, so I've learned to go within to calm myself down. That particular night was no different as my mind was playing out future scenarios of my mother's passing and imagining how I would feel and handle it. James was sound asleep next to me, so I sat in bed scrolling through my phone.

Suddenly an email notification came in, but when I opened it, it wasn't my email, it was James's. I was taken aback for a minute because I didn't know how or why his emails were on my phone. I hadn't ever connected to his email and wondered if he had for some reason, and as I scrolled quickly through his inbox, something told me to check his sent emails. When I did, the first sent email was an email from himself. "This is weird", I thought to myself. "Why would he send an email to himself?" I opened it, not knowing what I was looking at as I stared at a picture of a man's NAKED ass.

"What in the hell is this?" I thought, blankly staring at this random picture trying to figure out why he'd send this to himself. I knew this picture wasn't him, and I immediately started making up justifications in my mind. Then, I proceeded to check the rest of his sent emails and saw that there were emails to an "AOL" account that I never knew he had.

"I wonder if he's stupid enough to use the same password for the AOL account that he uses for everything?" I quickly connected to the AOL mail login, entered in the AOL email address that I had found in his Gmail account, entered in the password he always uses, and BAM – pandoras box had opened and a flurry of emails were presented to me. My throat felt like it was closing as I went further down this rabbit hole, reading email after email trying to figure out what I was reading. There were exchanges from him to all different types of men that went as far back as 2012 talking about things that just couldn't be real.

"His email must've been hacked. This couldn't be him. This couldn't be my husband. He's so big and manly. He's been with women before me." I kept telling myself as I opened each email, each one even worse than the last.

My heart was beating so fast. I felt like it was in my throat, and I could feel myself wanting to vomit as I read through hundreds of email exchanges from my husband to men from Craigslist and from men that I now refer to as his 'usuals'. Later I would find that he was on Grinder (an app where men go to meet other men to 'hook-up' with single, married, gay, or straight, it seemed as if it didn't matter on this app). I didn't even know what most of these emails were referring to, but I know they were incriminating, as my husband admitted several times in the emails to have met some of these men already.

I sat on the bed for one hour reading through the emails about rim jobs, blowjobs, poppers, detailed scenarios about a gang rape in a forest, my husband prostituting himself, and paying other men as young as eighteen-years-old or "twinks" as he would call them, to service him. He told these men that he would wear my 'panties' if and when they met up. He met up with random men that he didn't know on my birthday, our anniversary, on our vacations, and even worse at times with no condom. There were even detailed exchanges about bestiality with a dog. I was crying so hard that I was hyperventilating, still not wanting to believe that this was real.

That is, until I came across an email from my husband giving another random man, he just met online the address to our other home, for this man to meet up and service him. That was it for me. I knew for sure this was him and this was real. There was no denying any of it at this point.

-----Original Message-----
From:
To:

Sent: Sat, Jan 3, 2015 11:46 AM
Subject: Re: If you get jealous...

I always want to fuck you. Not sure I can today.

Mike

On Jan 3, 2015, at 8:39 AM, wrote:

> let me know if you want to come over and fuck me again

Sent: Sat, Nov 11, 2017 11:38 AM
Subject: Re: 2/2

It varies... not very often though.... all depends on what my wife is doing.... free now while she's getting hair done.... sometimes during the week after 6 when she goes to dinner with her friend

Sent from AOL Mobile Mail

-----Original Message-----

To:

Sent: Sat, Nov 11, 2017 11:33 AM
Subject: 2/2

What free times do you have now that you are back to work?

-----Original Message-----
From:
To:

Sent: Mon, Aug 12, 2019 08:51 AM
Subject: Re: Sunday

Free today?

-----Original Message-----
From:

To:
Sent: Sat, Aug 3, 2019 12:52 PM
Subject: Sunday

I need your ass to fuck tomorrow.... say your going to gym between noon and 8pm and come over....

Sent from my iPhone

Sounds wonderful. Where do you host ? I'm in Elyria.

On Dec 20, 2017 4:01 PM,

wrote:
> I have a very nice cock you can suck... if you want I can wear a pair of my wife's panties... gl, muscular, thick 8c, 43
>
> Sent from AOL Mobile Mail

Original craigslist post:

About craigslist mail:

Please flag unwanted messages (spam,

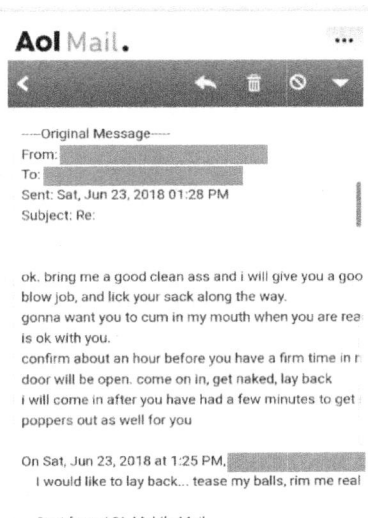

-----Original Message-----
From:
To:
Sent: Sat, Jun 23, 2018 01:28 PM
Subject: Re:

ok. bring me a good clean ass and i will give you a goo
blow job, and lick your sack along the way.
gonna want you to cum in my mouth when you are rea
is ok with you.
confirm about an hour before you have a firm time in r
door will be open. come on in, get naked, lay back
i will come in after you have had a few minutes to get
poppers out as well for you

On Sat, Jun 23, 2018 at 1:25 PM,
I would like to lay back... tease my balls, rim me real

Sent from AOL Mobile Mail

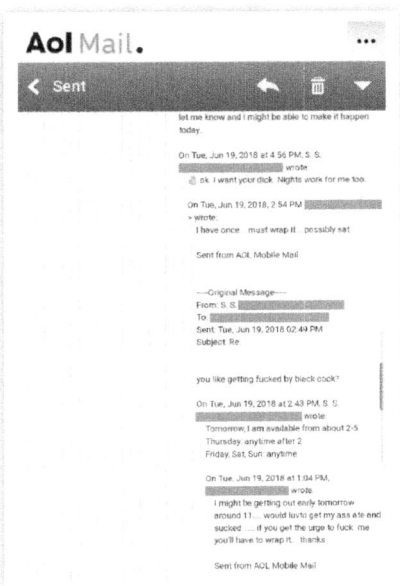

let me know and I might be able to make it happen today.

On Tue, Jun 19, 2018 at 4:56 PM, S. S.
wrote
ok. I want your dick. Nights work for me too.

On Tue, Jun 19, 2018, 2:54 PM
wrote:
I have once... must wrap it... possibly sat

Sent from AOL Mobile Mail

-----Original Message-----
From: S. S.
To:
Sent: Tue, Jun 19, 2018 02:44 PM
Subject: Re:

you like getting fucked by black cock?

On Tue, Jun 19, 2018 at 2:43 PM, S. S.
wrote
Tomorrow, I am available from about 2-5
Thursday: anytime after 2
Friday, Sat, Sun: anytime

On Tue, Jun 19, 2018 at 1:04 PM,
wrote
I might be getting out early tomorrow
around 11... would luv to get my ass ate and
sucked ..... if you get the urge to fuck me
you'll have to wrap it.. thanks

Sent from AOL Mobile Mail

"How could you, you disgusting asshole?! How could you?!" I screamed at him repeatedly as I hit him while he laid there sleeping.

"What's wrong?!" He yelled as he jumped out of bed in a state of confusion.

"What happened to your mom?" He kept asking as I was sobbing trying to get out what I had discovered.

"I know everything James! I know your disgusting fucking secret! How could you do this to me? Who the fuck are you!"

"What are you talking about? I don't know what you're talking about!" He repeatedly denied.

I quickly opened up the first email and started reading it to him. His mouth fell opened and his face turned white. He was speechless. As I continued to read the emails, screaming out loud and crying, he slowly started backing himself up and sat on the corner of the bed; this 6'4" man was now so small but still denying everything I am saying to him.

I felt no pity, no remorse. I did not care what explanation he had for what he did. All I could think was that I have HIV or possibly some other STD. Within one hour my husband, the love of my life, had completely turned into a monster that I didn't know at all. I grabbed his phone and started going through it as he continued to tell me it wasn't true, his email must have been hacked......... blah blah blah.

There was an app called "KeepSafe" on his phone that I couldn't open without a passcode.

"What is it?!" I demanded as I shoved his phone in his face.

"I don't know. Cindy. I don't know."

We went back and forth until he finally gave it up and told me. I opened the app to find pictures and videos of gay porn, and once again I couldn't breathe.

"I want you out of my fucking house now! Do you understand me?!"

"Please listen to me?!"

"Get out of my fucking house now!" I screamed at the top of my lungs as I stood up from the bed. I picked up his sound machine and threw it at him, missing his head by inches.

He left the room without a fight, and I could hear him getting into the alcohol bottles downstairs. I sat at the edge of the bed paralyzed from shock, completely numb as if I had experienced a total emotional lobotomy. All the love, the feelings created from years of memories with him, the connection between us had been sucked out of me and replaced with sheer hatred and disgust.

I do not know how long I sat there. It must've been hours, and then I remembered the gun that we had in the house. I quickly shot up and scurried around our bedroom looking for it. I knew he was downstairs drinking and thought that he could have the gun and come upstairs and kill me or both of us for that matter. I couldn't find it anywhere and had no choice but to venture downstairs to see if I could find it down there or if he had it.

I walked downstairs to find him passed out on the floor with an empty gallon of tequila next to him and another empty bottle of rum nearby. I hoped he had died, but I saw his stomach moving from his breathing. I grabbed my dog and walked outside. I dialed his sister's phone number expecting her and her husband who was a sheriff to come get him. They only lived forty-five minutes away, and I knew that was the best way to get him out of my house. I couldn't find the gun and knew that this was pretty serious. The response I got from her was the opposite of what I expected.

"Oh honey, I am so sorry. I wish we could come get him but we're so far away."

I took the phone from my ear in shock once again. I felt like I was being hit in the face with a huge dose of reality. Looking back now, I think she knew this whole time what was going on. It was so apparent in her tone and response. She wasn't shocked at all, then her excuse for not coming....... really?? Her brother could choke on his vomit and die, and she didn't seem to be concerned at all. Her advice was to lock myself in my room and wait it out until he woke up so we could work it out. I stood outside of my house wondering "who else knew?".

CHAPTER 3

NO LAUGHING MATTER

> *Betrayal can be extremely painful, but it's up to you how much that pain damages you permanently.*
>
> — **Emily V. Gordon**

What do you do when your reality is shattered and everything you thought was real is destroyed? What does real even mean- what is it? This has been a question that I often ponder since this betrayal. Do you ever truly know a person? Being betrayed is not the worst feeling but it's everything that comes with it; it is the feeling of not being able to trust yourself with yourself. Would I ever be able to trust my intuition and decisions that I make?

There were hundreds of emails, each one was more disgusting than the last. They dated as far back as 2012, and I went through every one of them. A different man than the one I fell in love with was unraveling before my eyes, and as I read through them, one thing was very clear to me, that his urges were getting worse as time progressed. Everything clicked in my mind. It all made sense; the drinking that got worse throughout the years, the changed behavior, and the extreme jealousy outbursts for no reason especially when he drank.

Desperate to get his drunken unconscious body out of my house, I called my neighbors for help. I couldn't gather the strength to call the ambulance myself for him, because if the truth were told, I didn't care if he lived or died choking on his own vomit. What I cared about was him not shooting me with the gun I still couldn't find if he did wake up. My neighbor was in shock as I told her and her husband what had happened, and I can't imagine how I must've looked. I had been up all-night reading through the emails and crying. My body was shaking out of disbelief; and as I was saying out loud to someone outside the family what had happened, the reality of it all kicked in, and my anxiety started to take over and I could feel my throat closing, slowly cutting off my air. She hugged me while I cried, gasping for breaths, while her husband tried to wake James up. His breath was shallow and rattling - this was not something new when he drank too much, but this time he wasn't waking up.

Thankfully, they relieved me of the burden of calling the ambulance for him. Two police officers arrived with the ambulance, and they went through his pockets to look for his driver's license and they ended up finding the loaded gun. It felt like my heart jumped out of my chest when they told me because I knew what he would've done if he didn't pass out first from the alcohol. I watched them cart his unconscious body out of the house, still in a state of pure confusion, thinking to myself, "How the fuck did we get here?" By this time my daughter had arrived and was comforting me. For the first time during the early morning hours, I was able to crawl into my bed, curl into a ball, and make a feeble attempt to sleep and try to wake up from what I had hoped was a nightmare. This is when the question of, "What is real," entered my mind. How could the person I considered the love of my life be completely different behind my back, living a whole other life, speaking nothing but lies to me? Was the entire relationship an act? These questions plagued me for weeks on end that eventually led me to therapy of self-discovery.

I'm not even sure if I slept or for how long. I didn't care what happened to him or where he was going after he was released from the hospital. That is, until I received a text from his sister saying that he might have to go on life support and asked me to sign over my rights in making medical decisions for him over to one of his sons. I immediately changed and headed for the hospital feeling hopeful that this was my opportunity to put an end to this awful human being from doing this to anyone else. I understood why she was asking me to sign over my rights because the truth couldn't be more obvious. I am convinced that she had known his secret this whole time.

I walked into his hospital room and saw the glares of his sister, her friend, and his eldest son. I felt their energy, and knew that somehow in this whole situation, in their eyes, I was the bad guy because of my refusal to sign over my rights. Once again, I was misunderstood, but for the first time in my life, I didn't care. The hurt and pain from his betrayal had completely taken over and nothing else was relevant except for the fear of having an STD or worse, HIV, from him. I was anxious to speak to the doctor about getting him tested. I sat across from his bed, in the corner, waiting for the doctor while on my phone, trying to distract myself from the fact that I was in the room with a man I considered the devil and his supporters.

As soon as the doctor came in, I ushered him into the hallway to speak in private. I quickly gave him a rundown of the story since he didn't know and asked in the nicest yet firmest tone that I could muster if the hospital could test him because the blood work I had taken earlier that morning would take several days if not a week to come back. He agreed to have a full panel of blood work done on him for STDs and HIV. It still took a whole day to get the results, and the waiting game for those results were some of the hardest hours. I had visions of the things I read in the email exchanges with other men. My stomach couldn't keep food down and churned at the thought of him not even thinking of wearing a condom for my sake, at the very least. In an attempt to release the tangle of emotions I was feeling, I laid on my bed and started journaling what turned out to be a letter to him. Right when it happened:

1/3/2015-08/27/2019

1,697 days of lies. Four years, 7 months, 25 days of lies. 1697 of you putting me at risk of serious STDs, HIV, and AIDS. My life meant nothing to you and still means nothing to you. I am disgusted by you by your treatment of me. I did not deserve this. Why? Why? Why? You took my choice away from me. You may have taken my life away from me and from the REAL people that love me. I possibly will have to be on HIV medication for a while and get tested every 3 months because of your dirty, disgusting fucked up shit. You never valued me as a human being. I was just a convenient naïve cover for your other life. You didn't care what you were doing to me. I hate you. I read all of your disgusting emails with your last encounter being this past Monday August 26th. You were doing this stuff way before you met me. Why did you have to drag me into your fucked up world? I will never be the same again. I will never trust anyone again. You have ruined my life and instead of owning up to what you did to me you try to take the cowards way out by trying to kill yourself instead of facing me, your sons. your family, your friends. You had me so fooled. I feel so stupid and so disgusted after I read these emails. You had the audacity to fuck a man on our anniversary 8/21/19, you came to my dying mother's house gave me & my mom flowers and acted like you did nothing wrong. You sicken me, you're pathetic. All the vacations we took to Florida you were fucking other people the whole time. Even threesomes with women and men, it didn't matter, black, Asian, or Latino, it didn't matter, and oh how you liked them young- twinkies as you called them. 10/23/2017 your father's birthday, Naples, FL after his birthday dinner you were frantically trying to find someone to fuck you. 2/24/2017 after your mom died. 4/6 my fucking birthday! 12/■/2018 your birthday. After your heart attack, the day we went to Hootie and the Blowfish. 6/17/19 At the rental when ■■■ and ■■■■■ were still living there. You let Chad, bare back you and cum in your ass in. How many others did you let cum inside of you? Aids, HIV, last time you got tested was a fucking year ago, September 2018. Every time I'd go to dinner, hair done, with my mom in the hospital, what the fuck is wrong with you??? Famous favorite question for Mike Hunt (one of your many aliases names)- "are you free?" Three to four guys a day. Meeting up before work, lunch time, after work- Did you ever fuck them in my house? You are a male prostitute, people paid you for sex acts. You pay $70, $60, $80 what the fuck? October 9, 2017, party rooms, a guy in a rehab station??? October of 2017 - Man's Best Friend email - ■■

▆▆▆▆▆▆ I know you fucked ▆▆ in Florida. Eighteen-year-old college kids. Good thing I stopped going to the gym. March 23, 2016, you cross-dressed, calling other people "Babe". This is beyond cheating. This is master manipulations, premeditated, you knew what you were doing but did not care about who you were hurting. You have fucked my head up. I am dead inside. I wish I never would have met you. Our life was a lie. You never loved me. How could you? You only care about yourself. When can I get my next blowjob, my next ass munching, my next encounter with anyone who is available for your pleasure is all that mattered. I didn't matter at all. Everything makes so much sense thinking back. Now that I know what I know, your drinking to help you get through your time with me. Your outbursts of anger probably because I interrupted a scheduled meeting with one of your random dudes. You slept with men, women, college kids (barely legal), ▆▆▆ you are a sick mother fucker. You thought I was so stupid that I would never find out. I can't make sense of any of this. Why did God put you in my path? My heart is broken. I am broken. I so wish this was all just a bad dream, but it is not. This is now my reality, my life because of you. You took advantage of me, you mentally, emotionally & verbally abused me for your own sick agenda. You don't care that you hurt people, you hurt me. You probably only tried to take your own life because you wouldn't be able to fool people anymore. I think this was some kind of sick game you played to see if you could get away with it. The thrill of sneaking around, the double life, well that is all gone. You have been exposed for the dirty, disgusting, fucked up cum dumpster that you are. That is all you are. A cum dumpster to random men who care nothing about you. But that's ok because you don't have the ability to care or love anybody. You use people, you deflect, you make fun of people for doing or being what you are doing and being. All the gay bashing you did, and I would say, "How could you say those things, your brother is gay who cares what people are as long as they are true to who they are." You are a hypocrite. You can't tell the truth. At least your brother knew who he was, owned it, embraced it, and lives his life in a respectful way, a path you could've chosen instead of a destructive one, where you hurt so many people along the way, mainly me. I hope you're happy with yourself, proud of what you've done. Karma is a bitch, and I can't wait to see what happens to you. I don't ever want to look at your face again, breathe your fucking name. I will be in therapy for a long time because of you. Maybe on some level that makes you happy because we all know what you think of yourself. I am sure even after all of this you will still think you did nothing wrong. A coward can never own up to their truth or wrong doings. You think you are above everyone else and everyone is *going to protect you and believe you. Well, I have all the emails, pictures, and dating sites. Plenty of fish, Bicupid, Craigslist, you saved Big XL Dick videos on your phone. The truth will prevail, I just hope I live to see you get what you deserve. I'm so scared I have a disease; do you even care about that? Do you care that you put me in danger? I will never be the same. You ruined my life. I hate you.*

By the time I was done writing, my face was swollen red from crying but I felt my first release since this whole shit show started. I finally received the call from the doctor to tell me that everything came back negative, it felt like a huge burden had been taken from me. I closed my eyes and thanked God.

"What doesn't kill you makes you stronger."

Relieved from the fear of having an STD and HIV, I went back to the hospital to see him. He was still unconscious, but I needed to speak with him regardless of his state of mind. While I was there, I was told by his son's wife that earlier in the day his friend Craig stopped up and he made a comment that 'maybe he will wake up if we put on some Gay porn". His eldest son called him a 'faggot'. I couldn't believe that this was being taken as a joke by his friends and family. Again, I wondered to myself, "Who else knew?"

I had never felt so alone in my entire life. My saving grace during this time were my two adult children, especially my daughter, who sat by my side every minute of the day, my kids never left my side for the next two weeks reminding me to eat, shower, and yes to even breathe at times. Of course, I've heard of women being cheated on, but I had never heard of a man doing these types of atrocities while married. It was so extreme, that it seemed unbelievable and perhaps that is why everyone was taking it as a joke. The joke seemed to be on me though and every time I had to face anyone that knew him, the shame and humiliation was so overwhelming. I felt like I wanted to hide away in my corner of the world forever. I couldn't help but continue to wonder if I was the only woman that has ever experienced something this fucked up.

CHAPTER 4

INSANITY

"

You cannot get to the other side without going through the fire.

— **Cindy Kaywin**

"

There is an unseen veil between what is and what was. I had lived in a glass house built from lies in the land of make believe, and once it was all shattered, the veil had disappeared. My mind could no longer discern what is and what was, and in desperate attempts to make sense of it all, I retreated into the cave that I knew best- that is, the cave of empathy.

"There must be something wrong with him." "Something must've happened to him as a child to make him do such things to me." "How could he have done this to me and faked it all this time?" Are things that my mind would circulate over and over until I believed it, because nothing else made any sense.

I thought to myself that I had taken vows, "till death do us part", and if something is wrong with my husband, I must help him. The woman that was so angry, that was scheduling for a same-day locksmith to have her locks changed while her husband was taken out on a stretcher, had now somehow morphed back into the caretaker, the nurturer, the "let me fix it" woman. Looking back, I was experiencing severe shock and PTSD. I started doing research on my husband's behavior and read many articles and blogs about similar behavior trying to make sense of all of this, but the part that made me feel infuriated was that everything I read victimized the man and not the wives or families that were hurt and betrayed in the process. Where is our right to choose? Where is our sympathy and understanding for the long-term damaging effects this has on us?

My family was adamant about me being in therapy and seeking help, and although I had a therapist prior to the "incident", I found that my therapist was even more ill equipped than I was in dealing with such devastating trauma. I once again was on the hunt for a therapist, but it turned out to be a blessing in disguise. You can call it chance or coincidence, but I call it divine intervention from God that not only was my current therapist not a good fit but that the new therapist I scheduled a meeting with after many hours of research for the right one, had suddenly become completely booked. Sometimes when things are falling apart, they're actually falling into place. This therapist insisted that I see this other therapist in her office and assured me that if it wasn't a good fit that she'd somehow make room to see me. I was disappointed but thought to myself that I didn't have much to lose so I agreed and went.

As soon as I walked through the door, I instantly felt the connection with this new therapist. Our energies were aligned and after the first session I already felt a sense that I was where I needed to be and was confident that I had real support moving forward. Prior to this, I had found that I hadn't given myself time to process, because I was so used to fixing others instead of myself. I kept moving forward the way I always did but this time I had Christina there to help me, to analyze my feelings with zero judgement, something I desperately needed at that time.

Although he had moved into the home he had before we met that we used previously as a rental property and was completely out of my space- I still needed answers and desperately wanted to understand and fix him. "Did something happen to you as a child?" I asked him on a random call while at work after one month of him being released from the psych ward. He couldn't believe that I was calling him and grasped at straws to answer me. "Yes, something did happen to me, but I can't tell you over the phone." Was his ill tasted attempt to see me.

I knew better. God, I knew better. I mean, as soon as he was released from the psych ward after attempting to kill himself, he went right back to it like nothing had happened. I still had access to all his emails and social media, and he did not miss a beat. I continued to see it all, but somehow had become numb to what was happening and more sympathetic to him because my mind was trying to rationalize everything and was convinced that he must be sick. My stomach churned when I heard his voice. My body was trying to tell me that this energy isn't right for me, but I denied it and pushed through just to make sure that it was really fire that I was dealing with- as if I already didn't know.

For another five months I fought for a marriage with a man that betrayed me in the worse ways fathomable, that did not care if I lived or died because of his actions, a man that had no remorse whatsoever, and even worse, a man that continued to play this sick game with me as if it was a joke. This time, there was nobody else to blame, but me, and that is probably what made it even worse. Now, I had to deal with forgiving myself.

For five months I put myself through self-induced trauma, my entire body would shake from the stress and paranoia, especially when I was at work and couldn't get ahold of him. I had lost so much weight and was constantly sick to my stomach. I had installed a tracking app on his phone that he knew about that allowed me to track everything he was doing on his phone. He did not care- he still did what he did but in a "low key" way you can say. For five months I demanded pictures, videos, and facetime calls to prove his whereabouts and always the same reactions and conversations as if it was unwarranted- arguments ensued.

"What are you worried about?"

"Are you serious? I don't trust you!" I'd explain.

"You have access to my entire phone!" He'd complain, as if it was absurd for me to act this way.

I'd explain that I knew he could be using his desktop computer to handle his "business". For five months I was gaslighted, lied to some more, and repeatedly told that I needed to get over it already because he apologized. I was treated as if something was wrong with me because he couldn't come over to my house or touch me. He thought we should be having sex in order to make up and couldn't understand why I wouldn't allow him to touch me.

It went on and on and I knew the day was coming that I'd be fed up and cut ties and leave him for good. He still hadn't quit drinking despite my pleas and demands to do it for our marriage. I even brought him with me to a session with Christina, and when she too suggested that he quit drinking, he acted as if she had asked him to cut off his right arm. He was more defensive than ever before, and it was again getting way out of hand- my queue that he was covering the pain of what he was doing. He had agreed in the beginning of trying to "work it out" that we'd both get individual counseling, but somehow, he ended up with two different therapists. His logic was that one was for his anger and marriage issues and the other was a sex therapist for his sex addiction. I soon realized that this was his way to find one that would tell him what he wanted to hear. I was disgustingly shocked and devastated that when I went with him to one of his sessions with his sex therapist that he succeeded in finding just that- a counselor that sided with him. The woman therapist told me that what he was doing was alright, and that it wasn't OK for me to label things; meaning, I was wrong for saying he may be "gay" or "bi-sexual". Each word out of her mouth totally dismissed the fact that I was the one betrayed by his actions, just like the articles and blogs that I had read did - there was no accountability for his actions. All while he sat there with a smug look on his face as if he was totally absolved of any wrongdoing. I ended up storming out of the session and letting the therapist know that she was the worst therapist I'd ever seen based on the type of guidance she's giving her clients and should rethink her career path.

Still, he had achieved in making me question myself. I didn't understand what was going on. Why was I putting myself through this? Yet, I still didn't leave. Perhaps, I was just scared to accept the reality of my situation and start facing myself to heal. Scared to walk away again and start over.

That's when I found myself in my car, ready to end things. My head wasn't right, and I knew it. I knew that what I was putting myself through was wrong but couldn't understand why I was doing it. If there is ever a time that a woman needs her mother, it's when she too becomes a mother and when she finds herself at the crossroads of her own life all alone. After coming to my senses in my car, I drove to my dying mother's house and threw myself in her lap like a child. There was no other place that I wanted to be, no other place that felt safe, but with my mother. I hung onto her with all my strength and cried. "I can't do this again. I can't do this again. I can't."

She stroked my hair and held me in her arms and soothed my soul the way only a mother can do. From that moment forward I decided that my life is way more important than what he did to me. My life means something more than him or the trauma he put me through. I found strength in my mother's presence that I was able to take home with me. I could finally breathe with ease because I now had hope.

He had an Arlo camera in his home that I had access to and something in me told me to check the Arlo camera app on my phone. It was nighttime and the camera faced the patio door in his house, and I could see a clear reflection of three people at his kitchen island. That was it. The last lie I'd ever let him tell me. His friends had come in from a 2-week trip to Ireland, it was the height of the Covid 19 pandemic, and because I knew they were assholes, I knew that they wouldn't quarantine. He wanted to spend our first weekend together in the same house to see if we could even do that even though he understood there wouldn't be any intimacy going on. I agreed on the terms that he wouldn't see his friends because they hadn't quarantined. My daughter had moved in with me who has asthma and diabetes and there was no way that I'd allow him to expose my children to anything harmful. He promised up and down, but I could clearly see on the app that his promises were once again just lies.

"What are you doing?" I ask him nonchalantly when I texted him as I'm watching them through the app.

"Oh nothing, just watching tv."

"Are you by yourself?"

"Yeah, I'm by myself."

"No, you're not James. You're lying."

"You're crazy. I'm right here by myself, watching tv." He

texted back, and I'd almost believe him if I wasn't watching him on the app through the camera in his house.

"You're a liar. I can see you on the app. You are with Craig and Casey after I told you not to see them before coming to see me this weekend!"

"What are you talking about? I'm at home alone."

"How fucking stupid do you think I am? I see you on the app through the Arlo camera you and your friends are at the kitchen island. I'm DONE. It's over!"

He did what he always does and got angrier and angrier because I was no longer buying into his bullshit. Then the name calling started, psycho, quitter queen, bitch. I agreed with him since there was no use in arguing anymore. I simply stopped texting feeling more empowered than ever. Relieved is more like it.

Within the next few months, I hired an attorney to handle the divorce, and wasn't shocked when I was told that he wanted to try to get alimony from me. Even though I was $60,000 in debt because of his spending habits, I decided to let my attorney deal with it and to surrender it all to God. I believed that there had to be justice that takes place in all this chaos.

June 2020, he came to move his belongings from my house as I sat on my patio with my arms crossed surrounded by all my siblings, with all the windows opened and my speakers on high playing every cheating song you can possibly imagine. I had cut all his shirts into sexy little crop tops for his fun encounters and turned his favorite snake boots into cute little booties for his cross-dressing shenanigans. Hey, I was just trying to help. More importantly than having him move his redesigned belongings out in the most humiliating manner I could think of in front of all our cul-de-sac neighbors to witness- I was finally free.

I still had access to some of his accounts and continued to check his social media and emails to keep up with his moves for our divorce and found Facebook messages of him to other guys calling me a bitch and that he's taking me to court for all he can. Well, at the end of the day, he got a measly $15,000 out of my 401k, because he was so anxious to get money. If only he knew that if he kept fighting and had some patience, he could've got six times that, but like I said, justice always prevails. In the end, God had my back.

CHAPTER 5

THE AWAKENING

> *You cannot pray your traumas away. You cannot run from them. To heal them, you must do the work and face them.*
>
> — **Jen the Rainmaker**

Where do you turn to for help when you don't even feel safe to turn to yourself? When the truth has arrived that everything you thought was real that was based on your decision-making, was not only not real but a complete façade, it is a scary place. You feel as if your mind has turned against you, and you start questioning everything that you do and everyone around you. "Is this person telling me the truth? Are they a liar? Is this person using me? Are they playing me?" Are all thoughts that consume your mind all while your subconscious mind is constantly searching for clues to support the fear behind these questions. Let me tell you, it is a full-time job living in your trauma.

I was beyond grateful to have my therapist Christina in my life. She was the guiding light in my life during this time as I sorted through my thoughts, shedding the layers blocking my true intuition, and started facing myself in a way that I had never done before- in the darkness. Before this, moving in the darkness was different. I maneuvered through it by staying busy; thinking that the more I achieved materially meant the further out I was. The truth was though that I never left the darkness. I had just become accustomed to it and kept trying to build my life in it, unaware that I hadn't moved out of the dark night of my soul. In my sessions with Christina, we analyzed and broke down piece by piece of how I got to this place; how and why I made the decisions that I made up to this point. I needed to understand so that I could give myself the grace that was necessary for me to heal and stand firm in who I was as a woman. With Christina's support I began to face my truth.

Growing up I never saw my mom cry nor complain. She took life's blows as they came, and she dealt with them head on and kept it moving. From the time I can remember my parents argued and they argued often. They argued so much that when they told me at twelve years old that they were divorcing, I was relieved. Their relationship up to that point had been such a burden to all our lives, and overshadowed whatever peace was in our home. My dad was a compulsive cheater and was hardly home, and when he was, there was chaos. So much so, that I started relating his presence with just that- manipulation, lies, arguing, and anger.

One late evening I hid underneath our kitchen table as my dad arrived home, neither of my parents knew that I was there, their arguing began the moment he walked through the door- I heard it all. He had a child with another woman and my mom not only found out but also found the picture of the baby that he had stashed away somewhere. She told him with dry eyes and nothing but sheer matter-of-fact strength that she had found the picture as she pulled it out from her breast pocket of her blouse and then quickly put it back. He demanded that she give it to him and reached for it several times and because she pulled away each time, he eventually ended up punching her in her breast where the pocket that had the picture was and grabbed the picture out of the pocket. I saw the entire thing. My mom did not cry. She did not fight back. She did not react. She did not do anything.

My mom was the caretaker for everyone ever since she was a child. Her parents owned a store, and at fifteen years old her father's alcoholism had completely taken over. He went from a functional alcoholic to dysfunctional, and her mother could not cope with the burden she had to carry as his wife which resulted in her having a mental breakdown. Consequently, my mom found herself as the only person standing strong in the middle of disarray, so she did what she did best- she took control and cared for what she could. Running the store herself while caring for her parents, it forced her to exchange whatever little childhood she had left for the full responsibilities of an adult.

While caring for my mom in the last few years of her life, her and I got to spend invaluable time alone while going to and from her doctor appointments and things of that nature. We spent this time openly conversing with no judgment about life and our experiences, taking our mother-daughter relationship to a much deeper level. A level that gave each of us an expanded sense of understanding and appreciation for one another. I think we both were a mirror for each other, reflecting the generational cycles and traumas, but ultimately a mirror that catapulted us to a realization of our truths.

My mother shared with me a family secret that she held inside her whole life, probably as an attempt to forget. But everything buried eventually surfaces. I learned the deeper reasons of why my mother was so desensitized to bad treatment that my father generously gave her for years. At three years old she was sexually assaulted by a neighbor, and not only did her parents know about it, but they also didn't do anything about it.

All my life I never understood how she never showed a reaction; how she never fought back. It all made sense now. The two people that were supposed to protect her, her parents, did nothing in the face of the most atrocious offense that can possibly happen towards their own child. It had been ingrained in her, her whole life, that bad treatment was just the way it was. Like many women, she learned at a young age to put a strong face on, the mask if you will. The mask that tells the world that you are alright even though you are crumbling inside. No one knows. No one can see the storm within because the mask protects you, and with time you even start to believe what others see. You learn how to forget what's happening on the inside, until, often for many of us, it's too late.

Still, my mom held no resentment and even continued to care for her parents, their store, then my dad, and us children. Yet, she never took time to fill her own cup up, to take care of herself. She didn't know what that was, and consequently, she couldn't teach us children what self-love, or boundaries were because she wasn't taught those things when she was growing up.

I reflected over all this with Christina during one of our sessions with tears streaming down my face as a much new appreciation had been given to me for my mother and how she showed up in my life the best she could with the little that she was given to work with. The feeling of shame for not understanding why I didn't have boundaries or know true self love was put to rest, and I started the journey of self-acceptance through understanding where I came from. My mom never remarried or brought another man around us children. She didn't want any man messing with us or disturbing what newly found freedom she was able to establish after my father left. She sacrificed her own need for intimacy and companionship to care for us, and it was always an attribute that I extremely admired about her. My mother has and always will be the hero in my life.

I wondered why I hadn't done the same as my mother given the toxic marriages that I had while with my children. Why did I have such a problem being alone as a mother even though I witnessed my mother being alone with us children? Christina helped me understand that not only was I battling with PTSD after my second marriage, but I also had created a blueprint for my life based on what I wanted as a child. As a child I wanted the whole family package. I felt the missing piece in our family of not having our father around by witnessing the struggles my mom had to go through. I created this blueprint in my mind that there was an order of the way things were supposed to go. First, you get married, then get a house, a dog, then children, and live happily ever after. Nobody gave me that idea, it was something I created for myself from my limiting belief and understanding of myself and my own traumas.

With Christina's help I realized that my entire life had been based off a blueprint created from limiting beliefs. I needed to understand how to undo this belief system that has kept me stuck and stagnant in these toxic relationships, feeling unfulfilled with myself as a woman. Christina started EMDR (Eye Movement

Desensitization and Reprocessing) work with me, to reprogram my subconscious mind. Through this process, it started getting easier to see the truth without the filter of my trauma. To organize events of how they really occurred instead of organizing them in a way that gave them a pass, through understanding and empathy. Unraveling my truth in its entirety has been the key to understanding my why's; to holding up a mirror for me to experience true self-acceptance through my reflection; to start changing what I wanted with grace and self-love.

CHAPTER 6

WHERE IT ALL BEGAN

> *The only people that get mad from you setting boundaries are the people that benefited from you having none.*
>
> **Unknown**

As cliché as it sounds, my unresolved childhood trauma continued to play out in my life as an adult, and the more I was able to recognize this, the longer I stayed as an active participant in my journey in therapy. I think a lot of us know this to be true but are oblivious or in denial to how much our current decisions go hand in hand with our childhood trauma. Self-denial of my truth has turned out to be the most damaging part of it all. I've realized that often in life we are the picture inside the frame, and unfortunately, we cannot see ourselves inside the frame. Often, we need someone else that we can trust to tell us what they see. It is a pivotal role that is crucial when attempting to change your wiring and decision-making process and is why I couldn't have gotten this far without my therapist Christina.

My blinders were slowly being lifted and I could finally see the exact traits and behaviors that I witnessed my mother make, were the same ones that I was doing as I trudged my way through my marriages and life. I never gave myself a break because no one else had given me a break. Really, I didn't even know what a break was because I never witnessed it. After my first marriage failed, I found myself as a single mother at twenty-six years old, barely making $22,000 a year, and struggling to put food on the table for my two babies. I refused to get on food stamps and be stuck in the system. I refused to ask anyone for help, because in my mind, these were my children and my responsibility. Despite not receiving child support from their father who was an alcoholic, I persisted. I stayed with my mom in the beginning and gave myself six months to save and get my own place- and I did. I didn't have much, and paying the bills was a struggle, but these were by far the best years of my life. When I go to my happy place in my mind, I go back to these days; to the walks with my children; watching them play at the park; stroking their hair at night as they fell asleep, one on each arm. No matter what, I made sure that I fed them home cooked meals every day, planning out a nutritious meal that included a vegetable, meat and salad that I'd give them, and I took pride in that. There were many nights that I'd go without eating to make sure they had enough to eat, and it didn't bother me at all. I knew that my situation was temporary and believed wholeheartedly that this too shall pass- and it did. With time, I received my promotion at work and with it, higher pay. I was working on rebuilding my credit that was ruined during my marriage, and I really felt like things were falling into place in my life. I was content and proud of myself for being able to stand on my own two feet. As quickly as things started getting easier, they soon felt like they were falling apart.

In November of 1995, my energy levels took a huge drop, and I was always tired. I couldn't stay awake the whole day if my life depended on it. I started losing my appetite and weight, and my already thin frame turned gaunt and sickly looking fast. At first, the doctors didn't know what was wrong with me, and I did not even have the capacity to even take myself to my appointments let alone take care of my children, so I had no other choice but to ask for help. My sister came to stay with my children while my mother let me stay with her and took me to my appointments. The doctors were running plentitude of blood tests, scans, you name it, they did it. I, on the other hand, thought I was dying.

I called my ex-husband who hadn't seen our children in months and told him that he better get his shit together because if I die, he is the other parent, and the children are going to have to live with him. I told him that if he didn't think he could, he better tell me now so that I can prepare a will and make other arrangements for our children. Well, he took that as his queue to come in and try to get me back since I was at my most vulnerable.

It was Christmas time, and I was too weak to drive, so he offered to take me Christmas shopping and used that time to try and convince me to get back together with him. I knew that even though I was sick, I had come too far to go back. I was relieved when I was diagnosed with a severe case of mono, of which I was guaranteed to recover from with time. Perhaps it was a test that I was meant to endure to see how bad I wanted my independence; how strong my faith was in myself. I think I passed.

Life after seemed more precious- it was better. I cherished even more the time with my children. I laughed more. Played more. Took time to be in the now with them. I wanted to be that mom that wasn't always stressed out or serious. I wanted my children to remember me as fun, as loving. I wanted to be the hero in their story.

CHAPTER 7

MY BIGGEST REGRET

> *If you had to relive your life exactly as it was, same successes and failures, same happiness, same miseries, same mixture of comedy and tragedy, would you want to? Was it worth it?*
>
> **Gavin Extence**

One small decision can often set in motion a string of events that can completely change the course of your life. Most of us don't give too much thought as to what direction our decisions have cast the wind to take us. We just go with it, eyes closed, enjoying the breeze and temporary warmth on our faces. That is, until once again, life happens, forcing us to open our eyes and see the truth of what we are doing. This cycle will continue to happen again and again until we learn to go through life with our eyes open, staying in tune with our intuition, and paying attention to the patterns of our cycles.

Out of all the bullshit I've been through with my third and last marriage, one would think that he was my biggest regret. I mean, I don't think it gets much worse than repeatedly being cheated on by your husband with random men. The thing is, I can't help but recognize what put me in that situation of vulnerability to begin with. Some things in life just break you and leave you wondering why. Why did I put myself through this? Why did I stay? When you know better, you do better, and some of us just don't know that we're better or worthy of more. For me, at least, that was the case. Sometimes it takes being beaten down and broken to recognize what you need to do differently in order to love yourself correctly, and yes, that means don't regret anything. Still, if I could rewind the hands of time and make different decisions I would, and my first decision would be to have never married my second husband- Anthony.

It was 1998, me and my kids were finally in a good place: peaceful, happy, and healthy. We had our own routine going, and life was looking up. I had one close friend who I'd get together with my children during the weekends. Knowing I was newly single and happy, she took it upon herself to give my phone number to one of her husband's friends who was a firefighter, "a catch", she said. I rolled my eyes and was furious because I had absolutely no desire to start dating anyone. I didn't want a man in my life, and maybe something inside of me was even worried about a man creeping in and me allowing him to pull the blinders over my eyes. Deep down, the truth was that I still hadn't learned how to trust myself. I didn't feel safe with me yet.

Of course, he called and despite how charming he seemed over the phone; I was immediately adamant that I was not interested. I continuously brushed him off and felt proud of myself for holding my ground and not caving in no matter how slick or suave someone sounded. As time went on though, he didn't give up, but instead, persisted even more. I don't know where I learned that it was "romantic" or "attractive" for a man to be that persistent instead of respecting the boundaries I created, but during that time it felt that way for me. The more I resisted, the more he persisted, until I finally gave in.

He appeared to have his life together, and like me, had been married before. He had a daughter close to the age of my son. More importantly, he was amazing with my children. They loved him and at first it seemed like he loved them too. He did all the things that pulled at my heart strings, referencing to me and the kids as "family", creating this vision that I always wanted- a family unit. All my life, I desperately wanted that perfect family that continuously was held as my blueprint for life, and anything less than that just didn't feel complete, especially when I had this man dangling that image in front of me.

I worked so hard in my career, building my credit, as a single mom, and was finally in a place that I could purchase a home. I lived outside the city limits that he patrolled. I however was looking for a home to buy in a suburb south of the city when he unexpectedly told me that we couldn't be together because as a firefighter he couldn't live outside the city lines. I was left with what seemed like an ultimatum. Either purchase my home in the place I lived, a place I could afford, or go where I knew I could have this family unit that we were working towards. As expected, I chose the latter over my much needed and yearned for independence.

The "catch" of a firefighter started slowly showing his true colors that weren't as he originally painted himself to be. There was an entitlement that started showing over time. Often as we were driving, he'd drive through a red light and when I'd look over at him and ask him why he did that, his response was, "I am the law." More times than I could count he'd ask me while driving what direction he should take to get somewhere, and after I'd tell him the way I would take, he'd take the complete opposite way of what I just told him. The little mind games to pluck away at my worth and devalue me were starting to appear- if only I could see what I see now when I look back.

Once we started to live together in a house that I bought in the city, the man that I thought was so good with my children slowly started crumbling before my eyes too. The thing is we hold onto that vision that was created to us from the beginning. It's the inability to release the vision when necessary and accept what is being shown to us. I know all too well that this is easier said than done, but let me tell you, the ability to make this transition can save you time, energy, and heartache. The moment my son ran up to me when I got home from work with fear on his face, I should've known. A red flag was being waved right in front of me, yet I fell into his web weaved from manipulation and words and once again felt stuck as if this was just the way things were in relationships.

My son is an empath and has always been the one to keep the peace. As a child he wasn't confrontational at all, nor did he have a mean bone in his body. When Anthony hit him over the head with frozen meat as an attempt to reprimand him for something he theoretically did to Anthony's daughter, my son didn't know who to turn to. He felt Anthony's energy and knew that there would be a problem if he stood up for himself. So, he waited until I came home from work and confided to me about what happened. Naturally, I was pissed but deep inside, I was more upset with myself. I yelled and stood up for my son to Anthony only to be met with his nonchalant tone and 'it's not a big deal' attitude. Everything I said was always downgraded or shrugged off like I had no point and was wrong. I was always the "crazy" one for thinking such a thing or speaking up against him. I was always wrong if I disagreed regardless of all valid points I may have had. Me and my opinion or needs meant nothing, even in front of my children, and even when it came to my children. My needs weren't recognized or noticed even when I was recovering from a tubal ligation that I underwent. He demanded to have sex regardless that I was in pain and was recovering, even after I reminded him of this. His behavior was that of a child that didn't get his way and was followed by guilt trips and put downs.

Why did I stay though? I asked myself this so many times before. When you're in this type of toxicity, it seems so surreal that you start questioning yourself. The ups and downs of the abuse, a mixture of put downs, manipulation, love bombing only when it benefited them, wears on your soul. When you're treated a certain way for a period of time, you start to believe that it's normal and start thinking that maybe this person is right. The truth was though that all he cared about was him and his daughter, but even then, I couldn't clearly see it because I was blinded by that vision I so desperately wanted, foregoing me and my children's needs and desires.

There I was in another relationship, once again, self-sacrificing and tolerating less than deserving behavior. Over time, that once charismatic, caring man was exchanged for a hot tempered, manipulative, abusive man towards me but only behind closed doors. To everyone else, he was fun, carefree, magnetic, and that's how he played it out to me too, so as you can imagine the transition to this other man behind closed doors felt so surreal. He was slow to reveal himself to me, and by the time I could fully see what was going on, I felt like I was too deep in to just leave. I kept clinging to the belief that there had to be a way to save this marriage. I couldn't wrap my mind around throwing away all these years, a marriage, and all the sacrifices I made to be in this relationship.

His daughter was an only child with an extreme case of only child syndrome. She would lie about things that occurred between her and my children and he wouldn't do a thing about it because he felt guilty that he and her mother were divorced so he allowed her to get away with everything and anything. I saw her as a child that needed love so, of course, I felt like I needed to compensate for what she was clearly lacking. My kids and I were very close and instead of letting him fix his relationship with his child, I diverted my energy and focus away from my kids at times to give a little more attention to her so she would feel loved. This eventually affected the relationship I had with my daughter, and over time it caused her to have some resentment towards me. I didn't understand the severity of my actions. I felt like I had enough love to go around as if I was a bottomless pit of love, but looking back I now see that I wasn't loving myself enough so that wasn't necessarily true. My love was on a budget, and my energy to be in the present moment was limited because my cup wasn't filled. I suppose this is how we hand down the generational traumas without even knowing it. My daughter saw more than what I did at the time and was completely justified to feel the way she did. If only I could go back and change things based on what I know now. The wheel of time continues to turn though, and with it, we all must learn how to focus ahead and not beat ourselves up for mistakes that we can't change. I've done it for years and it solves nothing besides hold you back from the experience of healing and happiness.

This is what abuse does though, it feeds off the confusion that it creates, then plays on it to keep going, all while disguised as loved, dressed in everything you ever wanted. And although I wasn't slapped in the face and physically beat, the verbal and mental games that he played may be considered just as bad. To the point, that I was so mentally beat down and drained that my once feisty, spunky self was gone and over time I found myself sitting there going inward, silenced, shaking my head in agreement, completely zoned out, and when asked if I had anything to say when he was done with his put downs, I'd just say no and walk away. I didn't recognize myself and had completely lost my voice. I wasn't allowed to have any sort of opinion, to stand up for myself, to have boundaries- nothing. Anytime I did, he'd find a way to tear them to shreds, put me down, and turn it around to make it sound like I'm wrong for it, and after everything was said and done, I was left mentally depleted questioning myself each and every time. In 2005 we eventually moved out of the city due to the change in residency laws that had been in place for firefighters. We now owned two homes, and when I say "we", I mean, I owned two homes. Both of our real estate investment properties were in my name because he still had property entangled with his ex-wife or so he said. I didn't want to allow that to stop me from buying real estate, so I went ahead and did it alone. We rented out the house in the city but after a year or so of us being in the new house the renter left and we decided to put that house on the market. That was at the same time of the housing market crash. We were now left having to pay two mortgages. It came a time where we could no longer do that and we had to let the first house go, yes, foreclosure. Since this house was in my name alone this didn't impact Anthony's credit at all, so he wasn't too worried when we lost the house. I, on the other hand, was left with this blemish on my credit and once again was left having to deal with the aftermath of my choices. I eventually mentally checked out and had enough and decided to leave in 2007.

I finally left with my children, but the peaceful feeling was quickly traded for the walking on eggshell feeling when I got a hit of reality and a dose of logic about my finances. Both of our cars were also in my name, and after doing some calculations I quickly realized that there was no way that I'd be able to afford everything on my own. In no way, shape, or form did I find it acceptable to lose everything I worked so hard for to this tyrant of a man. I figured that if I was going to start over again in life, it damn sure wasn't going to be from the bottom.

I sucked it up and went back and it was the biggest ego stroke of all time for him. After I endured the continuous verbal beatings, forced apologies over and over, the groveling for forgiveness, I then was told that I had to apologize to his daughter. For what? I'm still not sure to this day. Believe me when I tell you it took every cell in my body to hold myself back from telling him to fuck off. Over the course of my marriage, I showered his daughter with love and affection and even went as far to tell his ex-wife that when her daughter was with us that I'd treat her like my own. That is something I'd love to hear from another woman that was with the father of my children. Instead, I was given some fake words of appreciation just for her to tell her daughter on the phone while in front of me that she didn't have to listen to me, that I was not her mother. Nothing I did was right or enough, yet there I was, forced to apologize to her, which I swallowed my pride to do for the sake of ensuring my finances for my future. I focused only on the big picture and refused to self-sabotage it because of my pride and ego.

I never felt so unaligned in my entire life, playing the part, but I justified it to myself because the security of my future relied on me playing my cards right. My entire life I had been hastily making my decision when it came to my relationships, but thankfully with age comes wisdom, and I had learned the hard way that poorly planned decisions benefits no one. Life during this time turned into a game of chess, and I was very strategic with every move that I made.

The funny thing about people that display narcissistic traits is that they can't hide their true selves for too long before people close enough around start to see that something isn't right. That's what happened after I went back. My girlfriends knew what was going on because I told them, but their husbands didn't see it because he put on such a good act in front of everyone. I didn't blame them. I mean, the acting that he put on for people really did deserve some sort of an award. It was damn near impossible to tell between his charisma and charm during some gatherings, for example a breakfast with friends, that he was bitching and moaning an hour before about having to get together with "these people". But he eventually started slipping up and making off-handed remarks to me in front of people. I sat silent each time and allowed our circle of friends to see who this man really was.

"The supreme art of war is to subdue the enemy without fighting." **Sun Tzu**

I remained strategically silent and I allowed him to reveal who he was to people instead of me wasting my energy trying to convince people that I wasn't lying. On the outside, I may have appeared weak. I had let myself go over the years and gained some weight. I didn't upkeep my hair the way I normally had and didn't feel great about myself, and it showed. His brother and sister would make degrading comments about my appearance as my husband sat silent on the sidelines, but I knew how I looked and somewhere inside of me knew that this was all temporary. I may have come across as a woman that has been groomed to be silent-but on the inside

I was smirking, as I was hanging on to the light at the end of the tunnel. I knew my day would come. My end goal of getting out of that marriage better, richer, stronger, and wiser with the ability to live a better life with financial ease and freedom was that light. I'd think about all the things I would do, where I would go, what I would wear, the list goes on.

My daughter was already living on her own and my son was getting ready to head off to college himself, so I figured I'd wait to leave until then. The thought of living alone with him without my son in the house made me depressed. My son was the only one that brought me so much joy every day during that time. We spent a lot of time together and he always found a way to make me laugh, which was rare in those days. When Anthony's daughter went off to college, we took our time helping her get set up in her dorm and saying our farewells. Sadly, enough I knew that Anthony naturally wouldn't be so considerate when it came to leaving my son, so I had warned him that I needed one full day to mourn my son after we leave him. This meant leave me the fuck alone and don't instigate anything after we leave the college. Simple, right? Not so simple for what I can only see has a person with narcissistic traits.

Not only did he rush the entire process of setting up my son's dorm room, but we hadn't gotten out of the parking lot before he blasted the song, "Freedom", by George Michael. I looked at him with tears in my eyes, shocked but even more pissed off. That was the last straw, a sign from God himself if you will. I let him know that I was done. Of course, he thought that I was being dramatic "once again" when I moved all my stuff into my son's room and started sleeping in there. I don't think it really hit him until after I filed the divorce papers. To this day I laugh thinking back at the image of him, laying on the ground with a pillow under his chin, and he looked at me and said, "I don't think I'm going to let this happen", as if he had some sort of choice. I laughed and bluntly told him, "I don't know what you're saying to me because it's happening."

The loss of power and control was unbelievable to him, and in an attempt to grasp at straws he told all his friends that he could stop the divorce at any time he wanted but he chose not to. Finally, in 2014, after sixteen years I was able to sell my house with a good size profit.

When I left him, I never looked back. I was ready to move on with my life to greater and better things, but the one stop I missed, the same stop I always miss, was to face myself to heal from the trauma he inflicted on me. Instead, I busied myself- I was so busy getting into one project after another. I was caught in this energy of being constantly busy, really running from my own traumas, that I found myself months later vulnerable in the arms of the devil himself. Abuse is a spirit that can take many different forms. The damage and aftermath are real and lasting, that is, until you face them to heal them. Otherwise, the scars caused by abuse can lead you into a deep hole living the same cycle with different people.

CHAPTER 8

LESSONS LEARNED

> I was told many years ago by my grandmother who raised me: If somebody puts you on a road and you don't feel comfortable on it and you look ahead and you don't like the destination and you look behind and you don't want to return to that place, step off the road.
>
> — **Maya Angelou**

Life doesn't EVER go as planned, and often we find ourselves living a life that we would've never imagined for ourselves; in a house that just feels like four walls and never truly like a home; with a stranger masqueraded as love playing on our trauma. How does this happen? How is it once you think you got it all figured out, right when you feel like you have a grip on life, it feels like the carpet has been pulled beneath your feet and you're left on your ass once again.

I have always been a people pleaser at my own expense. I failed to treat myself the way I treated others devaluing myself in the process. How could I matter to other people if I never mattered to myself? I learned that these are tests. Tests meant to sharpen your awareness of self, all leading to one destination- increased self-love. With each relationship, time and time again, I failed these tests but eventually gained access to my self-worth. Ultimately, this is priceless because now although I'm in a place that I've never been before and I have no idea what's next, I'm walking into the next phase of my life knowing my worth, loving myself for the first time and with my head held high filled with excitement and motivation to stay curious and true to myself.

People can't hide who they are forever, nor do they have the same heart as I do, but unfortunately it takes time to see it. The question we must ask ourselves when engaging in any relationship is if this person is worth the time to see the truth. How do we determine someone's worth in our life though? We must learn to tune out the noise; the noise of our environment and their words and get in tune with our intuition and believe what we are shown. How does this person make you feel? How do they enhance your life? Are you left feeling half-filled or half-empty when you are around them? Most importantly, is this a relationship you'd want for your daughter or son?

I never want my children to feel helpless or less than who and what they are. I want them to set their boundaries and stick to them and never allow anyone to make them feel like they don't deserve to be treated with love and kindness. I never want them to feel bound or stuck to someone because they aren't financially independent. I learned through these relationships that you should never rely on anyone else but yourself to get through life. I learned to stand on my own two feet financially, and not to relinquish control of my finances to anyone.

Hearing my mom's story of when she was a child taking disrespect and betrayal over and over then watching the chaos and betrayal between her and my father without ever witnessing her shed a tear, I thought that is what a strong woman does. I learned how to put on that same face my mom did for the world to see to try to hide the truth. In reality I was hiding the truth from myself. That's the false concept programmed into us that keeps us stuck in relationships that do not serve our higher selves. We don't have to keep taking it. Strong doesn't mean you have to continue to allow people to hurt you, to abuse you, to use you, to manipulate you- you don't have to continue to take the blows. This isn't strong. This is the type of programming that we hand-down to our daughters that keep her separate from her self-worth and self-love. But this programming doesn't happen over-night, it's gradual where you don't see what is actually happening until that day comes that you look in the mirror and the person staring back at you is unrecognizable. I have defined the word strong incorrectly my entire life.

Strong is knowing how and when to say no. It's knowing that the ability to take blow after blow doesn't mean you have to. Strong is knowing how to let go and move on without looking back. Strong is knowing how to take time to be alone with ourselves.

It's knowing when to take a step back and have the courage to change the course of our path if need be. Strong is allowing yourself to feel your emotions, giving yourself permission to cry if you feel like crying because you have the confidence that you'll pick yourself back up when the time comes. Strong is not settling for anything or anyone that doesn't serve you. It's knowing yourself and knowing your worth through self-development and awareness. Strong is loving yourself first above anyone and anything else.

"Crazy is doing things the same way and expecting a different result." Albert Einstein

I had to put myself through years of counseling to break the programming patterns that I was holding onto. I had to literally learn how to think differently. I wanted different, so I had to be the difference. Learning how to set boundaries meant I first had to gain clarity on how I wanted to be treated by others. Once I had clarity on that, I had to learn how to enforce my boundaries in my relationships. Being a people pleaser that was very difficult at first. I had to be alright with making a lot of people angry and had to lose a lot of relationships, including that of my own daughter for a small amount of time. It broke my heart, but I had to remind myself that if I can't love myself how could I love her any better. I want my children to finally witness what real self-love is; what it means to heal. I had to learn to forge my path, alone, and to find happiness within myself along the way. Life is a journey of the discovery of self, relearning the different versions of ourselves along the way. I invite you to rise to the occasion of life and love yourself first.

A MESSAGE FROM THE AUTHOR

First, I want to thank you for reading my story.

I can honestly say that most of my adult life I've never truly been happy, now that's not to say I haven't had happy moments, I definitely have, but to say I've truly been happy...no. I have struggled with depression and an anxiety disorder since my second marriage. Decisions I've made and scary decisions people have made for me without my knowledge lead me to a dark place, a place I never thought I'd be but instead of giving up, which I was so close to doing, I chose to go to therapy. Therapy saved me and it continues to help me when I stumble. I am making my way to becoming the best version of myself with the determination of not just being happy in moments but in life all together.

I say all this because Mental Health is a real issue in our society, one I think a lot of people suffer with in silence. I want anyone that's reading this to know that if you're struggling with something in your life and you need help, please know you are not alone. I ask that you please talk to someone, a close friend, a clergyman, a therapist, a family member, or anyone you trust. God knows I know life isn't always easy, but I do know how you respond matters.

More importantly YOU MATTER!!!

Putting my story to paper has been very cathartic for me but more importantly my hope is that my story will inspire at least one woman to stand up for herself when in a difficult situation. Demand better for yourself. All of you smart, brave, strong, and beautiful women need to know that loving yourself more than another person or relationship is key to a more fulfilling life. This was a long, hard lesson for me to learn. I never felt worthy of people or their time but in retrospect I now know that I was too good for some of the people I let in my life. We have one life, one time to make this the best life we can, and it all starts with loving yourself first. Please know that it's never too late to start standing up for yourself, asking for help, and most importantly loving yourself above anyone else. Make sure you fill your cup up because you deserve that. Don't let anyone dull your shine.

Everyone has a story some more painful than others, but all are powerful in their own way. Some of us have been to hell and back in certain situations but we have not allowed these things to break us. We've cracked, yes, but we did not break.

This has been a long journey for me. To get to the point where I am today, it took a while, but I have learned from this incredible heartbreaking experience. I know this will sound odd but as difficult and heartbreaking that this journey has been, I am so glad that it happened because it has put me down a path I never would have gone down.

Again, thank you for reading my story, I hope it inspired you to never give up and to always put yourself first. I wish you health, love, happiness, and success!!

And remember, treat people with the kindness you would want to be treated with and spread the love to others.

God Bless

Cindy Kaywin

Cindy Kaywin Cindy Kaywin is a 54-year-old mother of two adult children who was born and raised in a small suburb outside of Cleveland, Ohio. She enjoys music, reading, spending time with her family, friends and attending, volunteering at her church. She is currently taking classes to become a certified mental health coach.

This is her own personal story of how she overcame years of abuse, trauma, and betrayal from the men in her life. Her hope is that by telling her story she can inspire other women to come forward, tell their story, get the help they need to heal themselves and move forward in their lives in a healthy manner and thrive. Also, more importantly to love yourself first!!

Cindy's upcoming podcast called, Love Yourself First, will be streamed on Spotify soon, and you can follow her on Instagram for updates. Cindy can also be contacted through her email or website listed below:

 ckaywin@loveyourselffirst.net

 www.loveyourselffirst.net

 love_yourself_first_llc

Made in the USA
Middletown, DE
01 May 2022